A Date with Destiny: It's Hot and Heavy

By

J. Maria Merrills

Publisher: 2M Entertainments, LLC

A Date with Destiny: It's Hot and Heavy Live Performance!!!!
Coming **May 2016** to Amazon Instant Video
Listen to a **dramatic reading** on Audible.com   Coming May 2016

Published in 2016 by 2M Entertainments, LLC

© J. Maria Merrills 2005 PAu002959969 / 2005-04-11

All rights reserved. No part of this publication may be reproduced or transmitted in any form or by any means, electronic or mechanical, including photocopying, recording, or any information storage or retrieval system, without prior permission in writing from the publisher.

All characters and story are fictional and not based on the lives of any real events or people.

Act 1

Scene 1	The Call
Scene 2	Healing
Scene 3	Church Business
Scene 4	After Midnight
Scene 5	The Bake Sale
Scene 6	The Date
Scene 7	The Bill
Scene 8	Revelation

Act 2

Scene 1	How Long?
Scene 2	The War
Scene 3	The Vote
Scene 4	Prodigal Son
Scene 5	In My Father's House

Prologue

Destiny's Story: Like many, Destiny is a young woman who struggles with her weight. Her love affair with food began at five-years-old when her father walked out of her life and her mother was left depressed, never fully getting over the fact that her husband was gone. When Destiny ate, she was able to numb all the pain that life had dealt her. Food became her drug, her lover, her friend. To make matters worse, she was involved in a terrible car accident as a teenager and lost the use of both her legs. Her lack of mobility only accelerated the weight gain. Strangely, all of those nights lying in bed without the ability to move gave her clarity about how she wanted to help others. Determined to be mobile again, she not only walked, she soared. The accident that was meant to destroy her had given her focus and clarity about how she wanted to help others and why she was put on this green earth. Destiny was determined to become a physical therapist and help others just as she was being helped.

Her hopes of becoming a physical therapist seemed impossible, though. She couldn't figure out how her mother could ever afford to send her to college, especially on her lowly single parent income. Thankfully, Destiny's commitment to learning, hard work, and good grades landed her a full scholarship to Virginia Tech. Accepting this blessing came with a price. Going to Tech meant that she must leave her clinically depressed mother whom she had cared for daily behind in Chicago. She reasoned that accepting the opportunity would allow her to help her mother financially, medically, and emotionally in the future. So, she left Illinois for Virginia and never looked back.

Thankfully, studies in physical therapy went well and without a glitch. Everything was perfect at school except for her social life. During her entire time in college, she was not invited on a single date. Of course, she blamed her lack of romance on her plump figure. Though she was beautiful, kept a sweet spirit, and a smiling disposition, no man ever noticed the very attractive, smart, capable, and ambitious young woman locked inside. Her fantasies about a slimmer frame started to interrupt her studies and her focus. What she wanted was a perfect life. In her mind a perfect life included a small waist, a fat bank account, and a handsome man on her arms. Setting away part of her scholarship funds for three years and applying for a student loan, she financed a drastic weight loss surgery during her senior year.

Now it is a few years after graduation. Destiny is 160 pounds slimmer and 23-years-old. Wearing a lose size 4, she has a wonderful career as a six-figure earning home health-care physical therapist, a beautiful condo, and a gorgeous candy-apple-red convertible BMW. The only thing that is missing is the handsome man she had dreamt about for so long. As fate would have it, she is sent on a house call where she will finally meet a man of interest.

Solomon, the man of interest, is home-bound, handsome, funny, and a young twenty-something musician who automatically has an unexplainable attraction to Destiny. In his boldness, he invites her to a romantic evening at home. However, it is on this date with Destiny that they both discover an ugly truth that threatens to knock them to their core. Though Destiny felt her problematic past lay behind in Chicago, little did she know about the brewing storm in Virginia.

The Play

Reverend Jacob Cross: *Pastor and founder of Ebenezer Baptist church*
Rachel: *Reverend Cross' wife*
Solomon: *Jacob and Rachel's 23-year-old son*
Destiny: *Solomon's physical therapist*
Deacon Lorde: *Head deacon at Ebenezer Baptist Church*
Goodman: *Solomon's friend, vocalist, and keyboardist in their band*
Sister Hattie Wilson: *Elderly choir member at Ebenezer Baptist church*
Deborah: *Destiny's mother*

Setting: *The play takes place after September 11, 2001 in Bloomsburg, Virginia, a fictitious moderate-sized southern town close to the North Carolina border. The Cross' have a lovely home and are living quite lavishly.*

Act 1

Scene 1: The Call

Rev. Jacob Cross and his wife Rachel Cross begin to pray.

REV. JACOB CROSS, a 55-year old reverend, is awakened from his sleep by Rachel, his wife, who is in the living room pacing back and forth over a disturbing dream. Jacob has gotten out of bed and is searching for her. He finds her troubled in the living room.

REV. JACOB CROSS: (*Calling*) Rachel…Rachel, are you all right?

(*Rachel is not responding. She is pacing back and forth in the living room and suddenly stands as though she has seen a ghost.*)

Rachel, honey, what's wrong?

RACHEL: Jacob, let's pray. Let's get down on our knees right now and pray. I got a bad feelin'. I got a real bad feelin'. Somethin' bad go'n' happen to Solomon.

REV. JACOB CROSS: Why? What makes you say a thing like that?

RACHEL: I had a bad dream Jacob. (*Recounting the dream.*) It looked like it was a rainy night outside. I saw Solomon's car in a ditch turned upside down. The wheels, the wheels were justa turning. Right beside the car were Solomon's drumsticks and they were all muddy and wet. The drumstick on the right was broken in three places and beside it was a piano keyboard. Strange thing was it was in perfect condition. The keys were spotless despite all the mud. There wasn't a scratch on them. That's when I saw you walkin'. You was walkin' with a little girl, only she had on a nurse's uniform. That little girl was giggling, and she reached down and picked up that broken drumstick, and somehow they came together, just like nothing ever happened to it. She handed the sticks to you and when you picked them up, your minister's collar came sailing down to the ground. That's when the little girl picked up her foot and stepped right down on your collar. The last thing I saw before I woke up was you. You had a single tear commin' down your face. (*Pause.*) Let's pray now Jacob. (*She hurries to her knees at the couch and pulls Jacob down with her.*)

REV. JACOB CROSS: (*Praying.*) Father, we come to you today standin' in the need of prayer. We come to pray for Solomon. Encamp your angels round him. Put a fence 'round his car. Protect him; be with him. We plead the blood of Jesus on him. We are askin' that our son be safe dear Lord. You said in your word that you have given us the power to… (*The phone rings and interrupts the prayer.*)

RACHEL: (Panicking.) Dear Lord. (*She answers the phone*) Hello. Yes. Yes. Oh my God. (*She becomes weak. Jacob comes behind her for support and embraces her. She almost faints. She hangs up the phone without saying goodbye.*) Get your coat on Jacob, we need to go to the hospital.

(*The couple grabs their coats from the coat rack and head out the door.*)

The lights fade.

Scene 2: Healing

Solomon, their son. Rachel gives some advice to speed up his recovery.

(The lights go up and Solomon, Jacob and Rachel's 23-year-old son, is lying on the sofa. He has bandages all over him. A wheel chair is right beside the sofa. Solomon is channel surfing. His body language says that he is trying to avoid a conversation with his father, who is seated in his minister's outfit reading the Bible.)

REV. JACOB CROSS: You bent on living out all the stereotypes of a preacher's kid, ehh? Everything that you got -- a nice home, good parents, and obviously the favor of God and you riding around town high on cocaine 'bout to kill yourself and your friend riding wit' ya, of all the dumb, idiotic, selfish, immature acts…

RACHEL: (*Enters holding a tray of breakfast food and vitamins.*) Now Jacob (*Attempting to quiet her husband.*) Sugah, (*Talking to Solomon*), we just glad you home safe. (*She puts the breakfast tray on the end table and bends down to kiss Solomon's head.*) Mama done fixed you a good breakfast. I want you to eat it up. You hear? Then get your rest sugah. (*She strokes his forehead.*)

REV. JACOB CROSS: You know the doctor said you almost died? They had to pump your stomach. Someone had laced that cocaine trash with Speed, made you overdose right there behind the wheel. While they were pumping your stomach, your breathing and heart rate stopped for over five minutes. The doctors said most don't wake up from an ordeal like that Solomon. Said it was a miracle you are alive today. The miracle was God, Solomon. The sooner you realize that, the better off you'll be. The better off we'd all be.

RACHEL: No matter how far you try to run Solomon, you can't hide. God has got a call on your life. Now you know that. You destined to be a great leader for God. The whole time I was carryin' you, you was such an active little thing. Do you know when I had my ultrasound; the first picture I had of you was one of you smilin'? That was confirmation for me that you would bring hope and joy into people's lives. Oh, you goin' to win so many souls for Christ. You wait and see here now. You here for a reason Solomon, and ain't not amount of ungodly activity going to change that. *(Pause.)* Now you eat up. You hear? You need to get all your strength back. I brought you some Echinacea and Zinc tablets, long with that Vitamin C in the orange juice; it should help get your immune system back up to speed.

(Solomon looks as if he doesn't want the breakfast, nor take the pills. The Bible, which was once close to Jacob's face, is pulled down to his lap as he looks at Solomon's stubbornness for a while.)

REV. JACOB CROSS: If you can snort that stuff up your nose, you definitely should be able to eat that breakfast that your mother went to so much trouble to prepare and take those vitamins too. 'Course you probably wouldn't have no problem taking none of it, if it was some illegal stuff now would you?

SOLOMON: I'm gonna get my act together dad; get saved; you'll see.

REV. JACOB CROSS: Look, now don't you go doin' nothing to impress me. God, he looks at our heart and our intent. Besides, I've heard that same song and dance every time we've had to get you out of trouble.

RACHEL: The boy says he gone get his act together Jacob. Now let's just leave it at that. *(Addressing Solomon)* I know you gone get saved baby, and when you do, I'm gonna be on the front row doin' my Holy Ghost dance. *(Rachel does a few quick Holy Ghost steps.)* Glory!

REV. JACOB CROSS: I'm not gone leave the boy alone Rachel. If he playin' with God, he'll go to hell faster than if he would have died high on that stuff.

(The phone rings towards the end of Jacob's sentence. Rachel goes to answer it.)

RACHEL: Hello. Jacob, it's for you. Deacon Lorde on the phone. Say it's important he talk to you right away.

REV. JACOB CROSS: I'll take it in the study.

(REV. JACOB CROSS exits for the study. Rachel gestures for Solomon to slide over a bit so she can sit near him.)

RACHEL: Now you don't worry 'bout your daddy. You know he can be hard on you. He only does it 'cause he loves you.

SOLOMON: Deacon Lorde probably wants to discuss my situation with dad. The church thinks they own me or somethin'; *(Pause.)* All those church folk, so holier than thou, casting judgment. Heck ma, I see half of them on Saturday down at the club where I play. How you think they keep track of what I'm doing all the time? They just sit there, front-row-and-center, watching the band, keeping their eyes focused on me, slipping a shot here and there on the sly.

(Jacob goes into the living room to gather his hat and overcoat.)

RACHEL: Where you goin' Jacob?

REV. JACOB CROSS: Down to the church to do some damage control. Deacon Lorde say some of the church members are down there talking 'bout finding a new pastor. They done heard about what Solomon did. Say it is the last straw of embarrassment for Ebenezer Baptist Church. Say if I can't control my own son, how can I be a good pastor to the church members.

RACHEL: (*As if she wants to discuss something.*) But Jacob…

REV. JACOB CROSS: I can't talk about it right now Rachel. I got to be on my way.

(*REV. JACOB CROSS exits.*)

RACHEL: (*Addressing Solomon in disgust.*) I done told you that your actions affect more than just you Solomon. I done told you that 100 times before. Yes, you are a preacher's kid. There is nothing you can do about it. Nothing you can do to change that. With that role comes a huge responsibility. You have a lot to live up to. We expect it. Your father and I deserve it. Ebenezer Baptist church deserves it. You know, you could be a role model for some of the young people; instead you out doing who knows what, with who knows who, and who knows where. Well I think that this is the last straw.

(*The doorbell rings. Rachel goes to answer it.*)

RACHEL: Well, hello. You must be the therapist from the hospital. He's sitting right over there. And your name is?

DESTINY: Destiny, Destiny Woods.

RACHEL: Come right on in Miss Woods. Will you be working with Solomon solely or will the hospital be sending others?

DESTINY: As far as I know, just me.

RACHEL: Well good. The accident has really taken a toll on his spirits. He is usually not so moody, always out and about, hardly ever at home. Now that he is bound to that couch and is totally dependent on his daddy and me, he's kind of snappy. He's absolutely hates this.

(*Addressing Solomon.*) Solomon, this is Destiny Woods, a therapist from the hospital. She'll be helping you with your walkin'.

(*Solomon is lying on the couch beating a drum pad. He doesn't even look up to acknowledge Destiny.*)

DESTINY: (*In an attempt to break the silence.*) Would you like to tell me more about what is hurting you the most?

(*Solomon is still beating on his drum pad and ignores her.*)

The talking drums, ehh?

SOLOMON: (*Looking up out of curiosity.*) Huh?

DESTINY: I said the talking drums. You see slaves were forbidden from gathering for fear they were planning a revolt, so they would communicate through a beat of the drum. Through the beat of the drum they would let each other know if someone were planning to run, if a woman had a baby, or if the overseer was coming while some overworked field hand was taking a much needed break. Soon master got wind of what was going on and forbade them from beating the drums, but do you know what the slaves did? They beat on their bodies to immolate the sound of the drum. Pretty clever eh?

(Solomon begins to disconnect again. Destiny tries to bond again.)

Right now I think your drums are letting me know that you obviously don't have a thing wrong with your arms.

SOLOMON: *(Begins an impressive jam on the drums.)* What does that tell you?

DESTINY: That you are good and a show off, probably in need of some serious attention.

SOLOMON: *(Laughs.)* So you got jokes?

DESTINY: Obviously your mama did too.

SOLOMON: I see you trying to cut? *(Laughs again)* I could fall in love with a girl with a sense of humor like yours. Oooh. It's my right leg.

DESTINY: What?

SOLOMON: It's my right leg. It won't move right. I keep getting' these sharp pains in it too.

DESTINY *(Moving down to his feet and touching them)* What about your feet? Do you feel this?

SOLOMON: Yeah.

DESTINY: Did they send you some hose home?

SOLOMON: Do I look like the kind of guy who would wear hose?

DESTINY: No, I'm talking about circulation hose. They'll help you reduce the risk of developing blood clots, which you are prone to lying on the couch twenty-four-seven (*She pulls the circulation hose out of a bag. Pulls back the covers quickly to put them on his legs.*)

SOLOMON: (*Suggesting she was trying to take advantage of him.*) Hey girl, shouldn't we get to know each other first before we do all this?

(*Jacob enters the house. Rachel catches a glimpse of him as he goes to the study. She returns back to the kitchen. Solomon and Destiny are too busy to notice Jacob enter.*)

DESTINY: I'm just putting on the hose. Don't go getting any big ideas. Now where is a socket? (*She looks around and finds one before Solomon can answer.*) Oh, I see one.

SOLOMON: (*Sensing the pressure of the hose.*) Hey that feels weird.

DESTINY: Something like a massage, isn't it?

SOLOMON: I wouldn't exactly call it that.

(*Destiny and Solomon pause a while and watch the hose move up and down. Meanwhile the doorbell rings; Rachel opens the door and Deacon Lorde enters. He and Rachel are making small talk that the audience cannot hear.*) They're kind of hot. Can I take them off now? (*He motions to take them off.*)

DESTINY: Oh no, they'll need to stay on indefinitely. You can unhook them to go to the bathroom, but that's about it.

(She makes some notes on a notepad and begins to pack her things.)

SOLOMON: I feel like I'm on house arrest.

RACHEL: *(Talking to Deacon Lorde.)* Yeah, he'll be on that couch for a while. The accident really took a toll on his legs. I'll let Jacob know that you are here.

DEACON LORDE: *(Addressing Solomon.)* Solomon, I have a few words for you – Just say no. *(Deacon. Lorde chuckles.)* And who is this lovely lady? Wait, don't tell me. You must be Sheila, Rev.'s niece. You look just like your mama. All you Cross' look alike.

DESTINY: No, no relation.

DEACON LORDE: You sure got that Cross forehead just like Rev.

DESTINY: I've never met him.

DEACON LORDE: Well when you do, look at his forehead; then look in the mirror at yours. *(Rachel re-enters to tell Deacon Lorde that Jacob will see him.)*

RACHEL: Jacob said you can come on back to the study.

DEACON LORDE: *(Addressing Destiny.)* It was nice to meet you, hear sugah? Say, you ever been to Ebenezer Baptist Church?

DESTINY: No, I can't say I have.

DEACON LORDE: Well come on out and join us one Sunday. We need more **good** young people. (*He glances at Solomon.*) You'd be a breath of fresh air.

(*Deacon Lorde exits to the study.*)

(*Lights shine in the study*)

Scene 3: Church Business

Deacon Lorde and Rev. Cross go over the church books.

JACOB: What is it now Deacon? I thought we got everything straightened out about this whole Solomon mess last week.

DEACON LORDE: We did. This visit is about money.

Rev. Jacob Cross: Money?

DEACON LORDE: Yeah, there is $53,000 missing from the church budget. The board knows that we are the only two who got access Rev and they blaming us. We sittin' on the hot seat, Rev.

REV. JACOB CROSS: It's not missing. I used it to take care of some miscellaneous expenses.

DEACON LORDE: What kind of **miscellaneous** expenses cost $53,000.

REV. JACOB CROSS: I used it to benefit the sick and shut-in.

DEACON LORDE: The sick and shut in? You know as well as I do that that is Deaconess Jones' department. Did you run it by her?

REV. JACOB CROSS: Look Deacon Lorde, when I founded this church 30 years ago; it was a struggle. We were meeting every week at the Chicken Shack, and we only had 3 members. Do you remember that? Most times, we were not even collecting enough to pay rent, lights, or utilities. That had to come out of my pocket. I struggled with this church and footed most of the bills; so as far as I can see, I shouldn't have to run anything by anybody.

DEACON LORDE: According to church bylaws you do. (*He pulls them out his suitcase reading*) See look right here, "All payment of funds must be approved by the church's finance committee before disbursement."

REV. JACOB CROSS: I didn't think the finance committee needed to approve funds that are used to help church members, only those who are non-members.

DEACON LORDE: Well, they do! Let me see your books. Maybe I could smooth this out before it gets out of control. (*Reading*) Sister Stevens $1500.00; Hattie Wilson $1500.00, Solomon Cross $50,000. (*Repeating*) Solomon Cross $50,000? Have you lost your mind? Your help to the other members is not nearly as much as the help for your son. He don't even come to church Rev. That ain't fair.

REV. JACOB CROSS: Look, the money did not go directly to him but his hospital bills.

DEACON LORDE: Rev. I don't think I can help you get out of this.

REV. JACOB CROSS: Get me out of it? I don't need you to do nothing. I told you once; I'll tell you again. It's my church. I can do what I want with the funds.

DEACON LORDE: Rev. see that's where you're wrong. It's not your church. The church belongs to the people. If all of the congregation left, you wouldn't even have a church.

REV. JACOBCROSS: That may be a blessing in disguise.

DEACON LORDE: What? Look, Rev. you're obviously under stress right now. Get that $50,000 back into the account by the end of the month, and nobody will even know it's missing.

(Rachel enters.)

RACHEL: Deacon Lorde and Jacob, y'all wash up and come on and eat some dinner. I've got roast beef, mashed potatoes, green beans, home-made biscuits, and chocolate cake.

DEACON LORDE: As much as I would like to stay, I've got to get back home. Rebecca will kill me if I don't run back home to that mushy meatloaf.

RACHEL: Well alright. Maybe another time, you and Rebecca both can come have dinner with us one Sunday after church.

(Deacon Lorde gathers his coat and hat).

DEACON LORDE: You know, I will take a few slices of that cake Sister Rachel.

RACHEL: Have it ready for you on your way out.

(Rachel exits the study.)

DEACON LORDE: Well Rev. you got 'til the end of the month. I'll be seeing you.
(Deacon Lorde exits the study. Rachel hands him his cake as he exits the house).

I don't think there is nobody this side of Virginia who can burn like you Rachel.

RACHEL: Deacon Lorde, you too much.

(Meanwhile the phone rings and Jacob answers in his study.)

REV. JACOB CROSS: *(Answering)* Reverend Cross. *(The audience can hear the voice on the phone.)*

REV. JACOB CROSS: Well, I'm working on it. I fell into a little snag.

REV. JACOB CROSS: Tonight?

REV. JACOB CROSS: Well, I can't bring it tonight. Look, I know I can have the money for you by the beginning of next month.

REV. JACOB CROSS: *(Pause.)* O.K. O.K. O.K. Where do you want me to bring it?

REV. JACOB CROSS: Listen Deborah. You bring me a picture or something. I'd at least like to know what she looks like once and for all.

(Jacob goes into his closet, pulls out a briefcase and starts to count $50,000. He grabs his hat and coat, dashes from the study and then exits the living room. Solomon was asleep on the couch but is awakened by a slammed door. Rachel enters the room in rollers. Pulls the blanket up on Solomon, and cleans the room.)

Scene 4: After Midnight

Rachel stays up for Rev. Cross while Solomon sleeps. He explains his tardiness.

(Rachel checks her watch, cuts on television, and finally falls asleep on a chair. Hours have passed when Jacob enters the house late, having missed dinner. Rachel awakened by the opened door and checks her watch again.)

RACHEL: It's after midnight; where you been?

REV. JACOB CROSS: Well, something came up at church, and I had to see about it.

RACHEL: It must have been something serious the way you left out of here and couldn't tell nobody you was leaving. You missed dinner. It ain't like you to come creepin' in late like this.

REV. JACOB CROSS: There have been some break-ins around the church. I had to make sure the church was secure.

RACHEL: I haven't heard about no break-ins. It took you five hours to do that?

REV. JACOB CROSS: Well, I saw sister Hattie Wilson leaving choir practice on the way out, and you know how that lady can talk. She goes on and on.

RACHEL: (*Giggles.*) I guess you lucky you got home when you did. You know that lady can talk the horns off a Billy Goat. (*Jacob laughs nervously; there is a long pause.*) Well, dinner is still on the stove. You want me to warm it up for you?

REV. JACOB CROSS: Why not?

(*Jacob goes to his bedroom with his plate. Rachel follows him out when she remembers the church bake sale.*)

RACHEL: Lord, I forgot about the bake sale tomorrow. I got to make those cakes and pies Jacob. I'll join you for bed when I'm done.(*Rachel exits to the kitchen. The audience focuses on Solomon's sleeping when he later wakes, representing morning. He starts to practice a few leg lifts.*)

Rachel re-enters the living room wearing an apron, looking fatigued and sounding winded. She has flour all over her face and clothes. She hands the cordless phone to

Solomon.) I've been up all night waiting on your daddy, when I remembered I had all these cakes and pies to make for the church bake sale. I still got 14 more to go, so if anybody calls me, tell them I'm not available. *(She hands Solomon a pen and paper.)* Just take down their name and number for me, and I'll call'em back.

SOLOMON: O.k. Ma.

(Rachel exits into the kitchen. Solomon practises on his crutches when the doorbell rings. Solomon struggles to the door).

SOLOMON: Hello Sister Hattie Wilson.

SISTER HATTIE WILSON: *(She has a pie in her hand.)* Your mama home?

SOLOMON: Yeah, she's home.

SISTER HATTIE WILSON: Get her for me, will you?

SOLOMON: Well she's still making cakes and pies for the bake sale. She asked not to be disturbed.

SISTER HATTIE WILSON: Oh, I won't be long. I just got back from visiting my sister in Philadelphia. I wanted to bring this pie to her directly; then I got to get home and get some rest.

SOLOMON: Alright, I'll let her know.

(As Solomon exits to the kitchen, Hattie looks around the room as if she is inspecting it. Solomon and Rachel are heard off stage.)

SOLOMON: Ma, Sister Wilson….

RACHEL: Now Solomon, I told you I'm busy. I especially ain't got no time to talk to Sister Hattie Wilson. You know that woman can talk.

SOLOMON: But Ma…

RACHEL: Tell her I'll talk to her later…

SOLOMON: But ma.

RACHEL: What Solomon?

SOLOMON: She's in the living room right now.

RACHEL: Well why didn't you say somethin'?

(Hattie has been hanging on every word the whole time. Rachel enters the living room.)

RACHEL: Sister Hattie. *(She goes to kiss her. Hattie backs away.)*

SISTER HATTIE WILSON: I ain't go'n' keep you long sister Rachel.

RACHEL: Oh, Sister Hattie, please forgive me. I'm just under a lot of stress trying to get these cakes and pies ready for the bake sale. I should have never promised to make so many.

SISTER HATTIE WILSON: Why didn't you ask me to make more? Or you could have had some of them younger members to help out too.

RACHEL: I asked some of 'em, but they said it would be easier for them to get it from the grocery store bakery. Young folks, they ain't got no time to cook.

SISTER HATTIE WILSON: Young folks, most of them too lazy to learn to do.

RACHEL: Well I would have asked you to do more, but I could never get you by phone. I haven't seen you after church for a few Sundays now. If I'd a known that you would have bumped into Jacob after choir practice yesterday, I would have asked him to ask you if you could have baked a few more pies.

SISTER HATTIE WILSON: I didn't go to choir practice last night, and I sure didn't run into Reverend Cross. I just got back from visiting my sister in Philadelphia this morning.

RACHEL: That's strange. Jacob said he talked to you for a long time last night.

SISTER HATTIE WILSON: Maybe I have a twin I don't know 'bout 'cause he sho'l didn't talk to me.

(*Rachel looks bothered. There is a long pause as if she is trying to figure things out*).

I bought you this pie.

RACHEL: Why thank you. Excuse me Sister Wilson. *(Calling)* Solomon, Call down to Food King Bakery; see if they can ask Carolyn can set aside 8 cakes and 6 pies and bring them over to the church for me by two o'clock. Whatever kind they have available is fine with me.

SISTER HATTIE WILSON: I love pie, but with my sugah I got to watch it. Lord knows I love me some sweet potato pie. The biggest sweet potatoes I've ever seen were in N.C. That's such a nice state. I almost lived there myself, in Greensboro. You know they have N.C. A&TT there. I thought it would be a great place to send my children. I think Jessie Jackson and Ron Mcnair, you know the astronaut went there. I don't know why anybody would want to float out in space like that; and why we want to spend so much money on space exploration. They should put that money on education. With public schools being so bad. You know...

(Hattie's voice is still being heard as Rachel starts to escort her to the door, forcing Sister Hattie Wilson to leave. She slams the door on her while she is still talking. Rachel goes to the kitchen and brings out her cakes and pies in a box.)

Rachel: Solomon, I'm going down to the church to get the table ready for the bake sale. Tell your daddy, hear? *(Rachel exits).*

Scene 5: The Bake Sale

Rachel and Sister Hattie Wilson discuss pies for the bake sale.

(Jacob enters the living room as Solomon is lifting his legs, but really concentrating more on TV than his exercises.)

REV. JACOB CROSS: You better start lifting a whole lot quicker than that if you want to get out of this house soon (*Pause*). Where your mama?

SOLOMON: At the bake sale. *(Solomon really gets serious about practicing some lifts)* Believe me. I want to be getting' out of this house just as much as you want me to.

REV. JACOB CROSS: Instead of putting all your energy into the TV, you need to be thinking about your future and how you can get your life back on track, getting you a respectable job, something' that's steady, something that will take you away from that wild lifestyle of yours. 'Course you gone need to go back to school. While you setting around all day, it might be good for you to take you some correspondence courses.

SOLOMON: I ain't going back to school dad. My love is my music.

REV. JACOB CROSS: Well, you may love your music, but it doesn't love you. You a grown man, 23-years-old, and you still living at home with your parents. When I was your age, I was married to your mama, had built a house, and started a church.

SOLOMON: Times were different then dad.

REV. JACOB CROSS: No, times weren't different neither. Being responsible is just being responsible. I don't care what generation you from.
SOLOMON: Well, when I get me a Platinum record I can do what I want to. I won't have to get a job that I hate to wake up to every morning.

REV. JACOB CROSS: You think you the only one out there that wants to be a famous musician? Well its millions and billions of kids living in the clouds like you who gone wake up in their 40s and 50s with nothing to show for it. Y'all gone wish that you had gotten one of those dreadful 9 to 5s.

SOLOMON: I'm not goin' be one of them. I'm gonna wake up in my mansion at 30 with one of my fine honey's right beside me, rolling in my Bentley.

REV. JACOB CROSS: You got a better chance of winning the lottery.

SOLOMON: At least I wont have to be nobodies yes man (*Pause*).

REV. JACOB CROSS: Are you calling me a yes man 'cause I pastor a church? Well this yes man put food on the table and clothed your behind all these years. It wasn't easy. It ain't easy being a preacher. Folks think we something other the human, putting us on a pedestal like we don't make mistakes. Think they can say anything to us, like we don't have feelings. People expect us to cater to all their problems like we don't have our own, problems too. I suppose if I had been home more often when you were younger, you would have turned out better. Yep, being a pastor means sacrifice and many times I had to be out helping others when God knows I should have been home raising you. Preachers, we are special folk. Not everybody could do what we do, especially you.

RACHEL: (*Rachel enters the house carrying some pies.*) The bake sale is going great. We've raised $700.00 already. Jacob, you think you can help me carry some of these extras to the kitchen? It was so nice of Sister Brown, and Sister Richards to have some of the ladies bake a few extra for us. Solomon, you want me to cut you a piece of something? I have your favorite --Pecan Pie.

SOLOMON: Yeah, I could take a piece of pie ma.

RACHEL: Alright baby. Jacob, I talked to Sister Hattie Wilson earlier today. She said she hadn't talk to you 'cause she been out of town.

(Rachel walks into the kitchen; Jacob follows.)

REV. JACOB CROSS: You talked to Sister Wilson?

Scene 6: The Date

Solomon and Destiny's romantic evening at home.

(The doorbell rings. Rachel answers. It's Destiny. She is not in her uniform and is dressed as if she is going on a date.)

RACHEL: Good evening Destiny.

DESTINY: Good evening Mrs. Cross. How's Solomon?

RACHEL: Good, as far as I know. He's been napping most of the day. *(Rachel goes to wake Solomon.)* Solomon, *(She shakes him.)* Solomon, Destiny's here for your therapy.

(Solomon wakes, rubbing his eyes and wiping matter from his mouth. He is being obvious in the way, he is checking her out.)

DESTINY: Listen Mr. Napping 'til Noon. I've got some new leg exercises for you today. Let's see if you can stand and add pressure to your leg. You can lean on me. *(Solomon stands slowly; he is in pain.)* All right now, lean your right leg, and let's hold it for five seconds. (Counting.)1001, 1002, 1003, 1004, 1005. *(Solomon crashes to the couch.)*

SOLOMON: It hurts.

DESTINY: Anytime you're trying to move forward, it's going to hurt. The secret is learning to press on despite the pain.

SOLOMON: That's easy for you to say.

DESTINY: What, you think you're the first person to go through something? While I was in high school, I got in a bad car accident. I lost the use of both of my legs for almost a year. That's why I became a physical therapist. Believe me; I had to go through therapy far more intensive than this.

SOLOMON: *(Mocking.)* I had to go through therapy far more intensive than this. You're not from the South are you?

DESTINY: Let's do five more reps, and then we can chat. (*Solomon does 5 more reps, and then they both rest on the couch.*) I'm from Chicago.

SOLOMON: Chicago? What made you come to Virginia?

DESTINY: I got a minority presence scholarship to Tech. I didn't have to pay one dime of tuition, plus I got an internship and a free summer in Ghana.

SOLOMON: Beautiful and smart. I guess when you've got that kind of package, doors open for you.

DESTINY: (*Motioning Solomon to stand with her.*) Now you do the counting. It will take your mind off of the pain.

SOLOMON: Hey, you like movies?

DESTINY: Yeah, doesn't everybody?

SOLOMON: Well, I rented <u>The Fighting Temptations</u>. Would you like to stay and watch it, (*Pause.*) with me?

DESTINY: I'd like that.

SOLOMON: Good. (*Relieved.*) I'll order a pizza.

(*Rachel enters.*)

RACHEL: Y'all finished already.

SOLOMON: Yeah ma. Destiny is going to stay and watch a movie with me.

RACHEL: If I'd a known that, I would have fried y'all some chicken or something.

SOLOMON: That's ok ma. I'll order us a pizza. (*He gets on the phone and dials.*) Yes, I'd like the Super Plus Pizza. Yeah, 2289 The Way Avenue. Forty minutes? O.k.

RACHEL: Well all right then. Destiny let me show you where everything is around the kitchen. Solomon, I don't want you walking back and forth. You hear? There is some leftover cakes and pies in there. Destiny you help yourself to whatever you see.

DESTINY: I just love southern hospitality.

(*Rachel and Destiny exit for the kitchen. Jacob enters with his coat, hat, and briefcase. Solomon is clearly in good spirits.*)

REV. JACOB CROSS: You're in a good mood. What are you so happy about?

SOLOMON: I got a date.

REV. JACOB CROSS: A date? How you gonna date laid up on the couch?

SOLOMON: It's with my therapist, Destiny.

REV. JACOB CROSS: You got a date with Destiny? Don't get your hopes too high. A young college-educated woman wants a man that can bring something to the table Solomon. They want a man with vision, a man who's going places. (*Yelling.*) Come on Rachel. We're running late.

SOLOMON: Dad we're not getting married. We're just hanging out here and watching a movie; but who knows dad, she could be the next Mrs. Cross. She's real cute dad, got a great sense of humor. You'll see. She is in the kitchen with mom right now.

REV. JACOB CROSS: Look Solomon. Your mom and I are going to church, but we will be back maybe even earlier than usual.

SOLOMON: You don't have to worry about me dad. It's really hard to make any moves with my leg like this. *(He shows Jacob his leg.)*

REV. JACOB CROSS: Even still, I know you Solomon, and fornication is a sin. The road to heaven is straight and narrow. Don't disrespect my house. *(Yelling)* Come on Rachel!

(Rachel and Destiny re-enter. Jacob is facing Solomon, but when he looks up and sees Destiny, he drops his briefcase, then his hat, and then his coat in an attempt to pick everything up.)

RACHEL: Jacob honey, have you met Destiny? She is the therapist working with Solomon.

REV. JACOB CROSS: *(Nervous and awkward pause as if he is marveling at her.)* Nice to finally meet you finally. I mean Solomon has told me a few things about you.

RACHEL: Y'all kids be good now, you here? *(Jacob is obviously nervous)*. Jacob baby you all right? You ain't coming down with the flu again are you? *(She touches his* *forehead.*). If you're not feeling well, you should not push yourself. You want me to call Deacon Lorde, have him introduce the guest minister?

REV. JACOB CROSS: No, No. I'm all right. I just got a little flushed. Let's go.

(*Rachel and Jacob exit. Jacob is last, but forgets to close the door. Rachel is heard offstage.*)

RACHEL: Give me the keys. I don't want you driving me anywhere acting as strange as you are.
(The door slams.)

DESTINY: Where are they on their way to?

SOLOMON: Revival. It's the only time other than the New Year's Eve ceremony that the good Christians stay out past midnight. (*Solomon leans over, stretching his arm around her.*)

DESTINY: Don't make me have to bop you in the head with that crutch.

SOLOMON: Hey, you don't have to worry about me. I'll be the perfect gentleman.

DESTINY: Hmm (*In disbelief*) Anyway, I'm watching you.

SOLOMON: What's Chicago like?

DESTINY: You've never been to Chicago? Well, in the winter, it is freezing and windy. But in the summer, it is awesome, the lake front, Michigan Avenue. the Taste of Chicago.

SOLOMON: The Taste of Chicago?

DESTINY: Yeah, each Independence Day every restaurant in Chicago comes to Grant Park and you get to eat food from any restaurant in the city. Maybe when you get better, we'll go. While we're up there we'll go Steppin' too.

SOLOMON: What's that?

DESTINY: It's this neat dance. You have a partner and you groove together to a smooth beat. It's like the waltz for black people. It goes something like this. Cut the radio on, and I'll show you. (*She demonstrates Steppin'.*) Why don't you try it. It'll be good therapy for you. I can hold you up. (*Solomon tries Steppin' too.*)

(*The doorbell rings. It's the pizza man. Destiny answers the door and pays the pizza man. The lights are off and the glow of the TV . lights them as they begin to watch the movie.*)

DESTINY: Cuba Gooding, Jr. is such a good actor. Did you see him in Men of Honor?

SOLOMON: Boyz in the Hood?

DESTINY: Jerry McGuire?

SOLOMON: Losing Isaiah

DESTINY: Rat Race?

SOLOMON: I see we're both Cuba Gooding fans.

DESTINY: Yeah him and Samuel Jackson.

SOLOMON: I like him too. (*Destiny and Solomon slurp soda and eat their pizza.*) Hey, did you know Cuba Gooding's father is a singer? They look exactly alike.

DESTINY: I saw him in an interview and Cuba said they don't get along.

SOLOMON: I can certainly understand that.

DESTINY: Cuba's father was never a part of his life. You don't understand that kind of pain, believe me. At least your father was around. I mean y'all are like the Cosby's.

SOLOMON: Looks can be deceiving. You mean you don't have a relationship with your father?

DESTINY: Relationship? I don't even know who my real father is. I've never seen him a day in my life. My aunt told me in secret that he might live here in Virginia.

SOLOMON: What do you mean, you don't know your real father?

DESTINY: Well my mom was married to a man I thought was my father for the first five years of my life, but then he found out that I wasn't his, so he split.

SOLOMON: Talk about drama, that's some Jerry Springer Stuff. Why doesn't your mama just tell you who he is?

DESTINY: She said he was a terrible man. When he found out my mother was carrying me, he told her he didn't want to have anything to do with us on the count that he was married himself and all. My mom is not one to stir trouble or fight so she left Virginia and moved to Chicago so her sister and brother could help raise me.

SOLOMON: Wow, I'm sorry.

DESTINY: It's not your fault. (*Pointing to his chin*) You have a little tomato sauce right there.

SOLOMON: Right here. (*Pointing to his chin with his napkin.*)

DESTINY: No, a little closer to the corner of your lip.

SOLOMON: Did I get it?

DESTINY: No. (*She takes her own napkin and leans in to wipe it herself. The two get closer as if they are going to kiss when the tape starts to jumble, and the TV sounds of snow.*)

SOLOMON: My parents and their prehistoric equipment, they are so scared about investing in a DVD. They are so scared of trying something new. (*Solomon makes a few adjustments and ultimately turns off the TV.*) Now where were we? (*They lean in closer to pick up where they left off when Rev. Cross enters cutting on the lights.*)

REV. JACOB CROSS: How are y'all supposed to watch a movie in the dark?

SOLOMON: Your prehistoric VCR ate the tape. *(Pause).* The revival can't be over that quickly. Where's ma?

REV. JACOB CROSS: The revival ain't over. I wasn't feeling well so I asked Deacon Lorde to preside. He said he would give your mother a ride home.

DESTINY: Solomon and Rev. Cross, I'd better be leaving. I've got an early day tomorrow.

SOLOMON: *(Desperate.)* Destiny you don't have to leave right now. We can talk. I'm sure dad has got to get in the bed and lay down or some things to do in his study.

REV. JACOB CROSS: No dad doesn't.

DESTINY: No, Solomon that's ok. I'll see you later *(She packs her things and exits).*

SOLOMON: You've got perfect timing dad.

REV. JACOB CROSS: Timing is always perfect when you're coming to the place where you pay all the bills. Well, I'm going upstairs and get in the bed.

SOLOMON: If you'd said that earlier, Destiny would have stayed.

REV. JACOB CROSS: Look, you need to focus on getting yourself well instead of dating, and jumping on the first thing you see who can wear a skirt.

SOLOMON: It's not that dad. Destiny's different. I feel a strange connection to her, like I can tell her anything.

REV. JACOB CROSS: I don't know about that. You shouldn't confide everything to a woman you hardly know.

It's been the downfall of man since the beginning of time. Look at what happened to Adam and Samson.

(*Rachel enters the house quickly.*)

RACHEL: Jacob, you doing all right? I could not stay there at the church worrying about you. You look like you were out of it. Good you came home when you did. Folks were asking me if you were on medication.

REV JACOB CROSS: I feel better now. I'm going to bed.

RACHEL: You do that. If you don't look better tomorrow, I want you to go to the doctor. (*Jacob exits to his room.*) Destiny in the kitchen?

SOLOMON: No, she left early.

RACHEL: Why? Solomon you didn't make her mad did you?

SOLOMON: No, when dad came in early, he interrupted us.

RACHEL: Oh. Ohh? You really like her don't you?

SOLOMON: Yeah ma. She's a lot different then most of the chicks I holler at.

RACHEL: You know, I really like her too. There is something about her. She feels like the daughter I always wanted but never had.

SOLOMON: She just might be your daughter one day. Who knows? We'll see.

FADE

Scene 7: The Bill

Rachel receives an unexpected phone call.

It is the next morning. Rachel is on the phone.

RACHEL: Yes, this is Mrs. Cross. It's late? There must be some mistake. Rev. Cross took care of the bill weeks ago. What do you mean, you don't have it? He wrote a check for it. No, I don't have the check number. Look, I'll just have to have Rev. Cross call you when he gets in. It should be around 6:00. Y'all are open till 9:00? Yes I have a pen and paper, (*reading aloud.*) 854-1200. I'll make sure he gets in touch with you.

SOLOMON: Who was that?

RACHEL: Hospital.

SOLOMON: Hospital?

RACHEL: Something is crossed up. They said they never got the payment for your hospital bill.

SOLOMON: That's got to be a mistake. You know Rev. Jacob Cross always stays on top of stuff like that. (*Mocking.*) Son, when you don't pay your bills that's stealing and stealing is a sin. God said thou shall not steal.

(*The doorbell rings. Its Solomon's friend from the band Goodman.*)

RACHEL: Goodman, what a nice surprise. I was wondering when some of Solomon's friends were going to come visit. I'm so glad you came out of the accident uninjured, not one broken bone, not one scratch. Solomon would have never have forgiven himself if something would have happened to you.

GOODMAN: God is good, Mrs. Cross.

RACHEL: All the time he is.

(*Goodman goes to talk to Solomon on the couch.*)

GOODMAN: What's up man? Get up from that couch. (*They laugh together.*)

SOLOMON: I'm just trying to chill like you do.

GOODMAN: Man, you know I can't stay at the crib all day like that.

SOLOMON: Tell everybody in the band to hold tight. My therapist says I'll be up and around real soon.

GOODMAN: You haven't heard? Charley ain't been by to see you?

SOLOMON: You the only one I've seen since the accident.

GOODMAN: Well, I don't know what is going on with the band.

SOLOMON: Why not?

GOODMAN: I quit the band after the accident.

SOLOMON: You quit the band? How we gone make our songs Platinum without vocals and keyboard?

GOODMAN: I don't know. My plans have changed man. I'm heading in a new direction. That's what I was coming to talk to you about. I got some new songs, and I wanted to see if you wanted to be in a band I'm putting together.

SOLOMON: What's the sound? R &B, Pop, Rap? (*There's an awkward silence.*) Awwww, don't tell me it is some of that Heavy Metal stuff. You know I'm not into that. That's your thing man.

GOODMAN: It's Gospel.

SOLOMON: Gospel? Gospel? (*Solomon laughs uncontrollably.*) Man when I think of Gospel, you're the last person I think of.

GOODMAN: Look, I haven't told nobody this, but something strange happened to me when we had the accident. I went to Hell.

SOLOMON: Yeah, it was a rough night for the both of us.

GOODMAN: Naw man, I actually went to Hell. I feel God has ordered my steps here. That's why I'm telling you. You see that night, I saw both of us laying upside down in that car. The only thing was I was floating outside my body. Then all of a sudden, I felt like a huge vacuum started pulling me down. I started sinking farther and farther down, 'till I was under the car, underneath the ground. Then there was total blackness; that's when the demons appeared. I was sweating and getting hotter and hotter. Then the demons started laughing at me, jabbing me. I wanted out. I tried to scream. I started to, to have a flashback. The one thing in my life that stood out was me as a little boy. I was kneeled down beside the bed with my mama; we were saying the bedtime prayer: (*reciting*) Now I lay me down to sleep. I pray the lord my soul to keep; and if I should die before I wake, I pray the lord my soul to take., In Jesus name I pray, Amen. As soon as I said the name Jesus those demons scattered. They were shivering. They were afraid of that name. Something just told me to keep saying it: Jesus, Jesus, Jesus. Then all of a sudden there was a crack of light in the total darkness. Man, the little crack it just lit Hell up like noonday. When I looked up I saw a man standing there. It was something about that man. He had gentle eyes and hands. I just felt warm and the feeling of total love surround me. It felt like my mama's hug. It was Jesus. He told me it wasn't my time. He said I had work to do, touched me, and then he vanished. The day I left the hospital, I went straight down to my Mama's church and got saved. Ever since then I've been in the Word. Solomon, I feel a high that I never felt on Cocaine, Speed, or Pot. And the best thing about this high man is you don't have a hangover; you don't come crashing down.

SOLOMON: Man, an experience like could make you live right.

GOODMAN: God didn't just allow me that experience to straighten me out. He did it to help you too, and to help others. God has a higher calling for my life Solomon. He has a higher calling for you too. You don't have to give me an answer about using your talent for the Lord today. You can think about it, pray about it, and let me know.

SOLOMON: Man, I haven't prayed in so long. God doesn't listen to mess-ups like me.

GOODMAN: Man, I was messed up too, but do you know what I learned? Jesus didn't come to save people living perfect lives. He came for the messed up folks like you and me. He wants a relationship with us.

SOLOMON: I don't even know much about Gospel music except those songs the old folks sing down at my father's church. (*He mocks the morning noise of the old folks choir. "Pass Me Not"*) That stuff just makes me depressed man. Make me want to just kill myself and get it all over with if I got to wait to be happy 'til I go to heaven.

GOODMAN: Man, that's old Gospel. In Psalms 33: 1-3, God said we should sing joyfully to the Lord, sing him a new song, and play skillfully. You got your drum pads? (*Solomon gets them out from under the sofa.*) Now play the beat to the last song we were just working on. (*Solomon complies*) O.k. now do you know *Stomp*, by Kirk Franklin?

SOLOMON: Yeah man, that's a jam.

GOODMAN: Well, hit that beat. (*Solomon complies.*) Now can you tell me how the process of playing the Gospel song was any different then playing our band's song?

SOLOMON: No, it was the same.

GOODMAN: Exactly. So you see man, you got a choice. You can use your drums to glorify the world or you can glorify the Lord.

SOLOMON: I never thought about it that way.

GOODMAN: Hey, now you know. We still can have that Platinum record, only this time it will be in Gospel music.

(*The doorbell rings. Goodman goes to answer it. Destiny enters and goes to the couch.*)

DESTINY: Oh, Hi.

GOODMAN: Hey.

SOLOMON: Destiny, I want you to meet my friend Goodman. Goodman and I used to play in a band together. We're talking about starting a new group.

DESTINY: Oh yeah, well nice to meet you Goodman.

GOODMAN: Don't I know you from somewhere? Did you go to Southeast High School?

DESTINY: No, I'm from Chicago.

GOODMAN: I may miss a name, but I never forget a face, at least not one like yours. *(Pause.)* Hey, I know where, Virginia Tech, African American History 100. You sat on the front row.

DESTINY: Yeah that's right.

SOLOMON: Destiny, aren't you here to give me therapy?

DESTINY: Sorry, Solomon. Let's start on those leg lifts.

GOODMAN: I guess I'd better let y'all get back. It was nice to see you again Destiny. Think about it Solomon. Get back to me.

(Goodman exits.)

DESTINY: Solomon, can I talk to you quickly before we get started? It's about last night. I think we're moving way too fast. When I left, I just didn't feel right. I felt funny?

SOLOMON: Funny? What you ain't attracted to me? Do you think I'm ugly or something?

DESTINY: No it's not that. Not at all.

SOLOMON: Is it because I haven't been to college? Look I was just thinking about taking some classes on the Internet.

DESTINY: No, it's not that at all. I can't even put words to it. Let's just back off.

SOLOMON: I saw the way you were looking at Goodman. You must have seen something that you like better.

DESTINY: Don't insult me. It's not like that at all. Let's just keep our relationship professional. Let's be friends.

SOLOMON: So it's going to be like that. (*Solomon pushes one of her bags on the floor.*)

DESTINY: I think we should end this session now, get some space.

(*As Destiny exits, Deacon Lorde enters*)

DEACON LORDE: What's wrong with her?

(*Rachel enters.*)

RACHEL: I thought I heard the door open. Deacon Lorde, Jacob's not here. He should be back later on this evening.

DEACON LORDE: Actually, I'm here to see you.

RACHEL: Come on let's go to the kitchen. I just made a sweet potato cake.

DEACON LORDE: A sweet potato cake? No wonder Rev. ain't fat. You can't lose no weight around here with your good cooking. Would it be all right if we meet in the study? I have to show you something.

(*They exit to the study.*)

RACHEL: Now what is it you want to show me?

DEACON LORDE: This. (*He hands her a check.*)

RACHEL: Why this is a check for $1,000. I thank you, but I can't take this. Why don't you donate it to the church?

DEACON LORDE: Rachel, I know you and Rev are going through a difficult time right now. God laid it on my heart to give you this check. You can put some of the money back that Rev took out of the Sick-and-Shut-in account.

RACHEL: What? Jacob took some money out of the Sick and Shut-in account?

DEACON LORDE: Look, I ought to be getting on now. Rebecca said dinner would be on the table at 6:00 sharp.

RACHEL: Hold up Deacon Lorde. You accused Jacob of taking some money from the Sick and Shut-in fund. He did no such thing.

DEACON LORDE: Yeah he did too. And I'll prove it to you. (*He opens the ledger on the desk*) See $50,000 was used to pay Solomon's hospital bills.

RACHEL: That can't be right 'cause the hospital called today said they ain't got the payment (*she catches herself.*)

DEACON LORDE: If what you are telling me is true. Something's up Rachel. What is going on?

RACHEL: I don't know, but Jacob and I will have to have a talk once he gets home.

DEACON LORDE: Now Rachel, I still want you to take this money. Put it towards your family needs. Now don't you tell Rev. what we discussed. I don't want him to think that we discussing things behind his back.

(*Deacon Lorde exits as Rachel sees him out. Rachel looks troubled*)

Solomon.

SOLOMON: Deacon Lorde.

RACHEL: Destiny sure did leave out of here in a hurry.

SOLOMON: Destiny leaving is not what has your face looking' all tore up. Did Deacon Lorde tell you something that upset you?

RACHEL: Naw. Just something about church business.

SOLOMON: Church business has never had you looking so frustrated. What is it ma? You can tell me.

RACHEL: Not a word of this to your father Solomon. You know how private he is. You know that call I got from the hospital 'bout your bill? Well your daddy ain't paid it. Some money is missing from the church budget. He told Deacon Lorde he paid your hospital bills with it.

SOLOMON: Now you know dad doesn't lie; he sure doesn't steal. There must be some misunderstanding.

RACHEL: No, something's up Solomon. He's been acting real strange lately. He's been staying out late. He told me he was talking to sister Hattie Wilson one time, but she came the next day, remember and said she been out of town. Then he getting all flustered that night of the revival. It just ain't like him to act so strange. I think your daddy done got him a woman.

SOLOMON: Dad? No. Now you're talking crazy ma. I'm sure there is a good explanation for all of this. And if he is, we'll just pack our sh...

RACHEL: Now you watch your mouth Solomon.

Scene 8: Revelation

Rev. Cross and Solomon have a confrontation.

(*The key is heard in the door. Jacob enters. He sets down all of his belongings.*)

REV. JACOB CROSS Woo, I'm tired. I've had a real tough day.
(*He sits down in his chair.*)

RACHEL: Jacob don't get too comfortable. I need to talk to you.

REV. JACOB CROSS: Can't it wait 'til after supper?

RACHEL: No, I need to talk to you right now. Solomon you go on and start your dinner. We'll be in, in a little while. *(Solomon exits to the kitchen, hobbling.)* I think it would be best if we talk in the study.

(Rachel and Jacob exit to the study.).

REV. JACOB CROSS: What is it Rachel?

RACHEL: Jacob Anotonio Cross, you've been acting real strange lately, and I want to know what it is. I want to know what is going on.

REV. JACOB CROSS: Ain't nothing going on.

RACHEL: Yes it is too. I'm talking about the late nights; the lie you told about talking to Hattie Wilson, and the $50,000 you took from the Sick-and-Shut in fund to pay Solomon's hospital bills. News Flash, the hospital called and the bill ain't been paid.

REV. JACOB CROSS: Well who told you about the Sick-and-Shut in Fund? *(Pause)* Deacon Lorde. Lorde knows everything.

RACHEL: Well.

REV. JACOB CROSS: Well what?

RACHEL: I'm waiting on your explanation.

REV. JACOB CROSS: There is no explanation.

RACHEL: All those events are no coincidence. There is something going on. I know you. You can't fool me. I've been married to you for 24 years, so I know when something is wrong Jacob. And believe you me, its better for you to tell me than if I have to find out from someone else. Is it another woman?

(*The doorbell rings it's Deacon Lord. Rachel Answers.*)

DEACON LORDE: Rev. home yet?

RACHEL: Yes, he's in the study.

DEACON LORDE: Rachel, I just got a call on my cell. All hell breaking lose down at the church. I turned right back around so I could tell you in person. Folks done found out that he took the money. They want his resignation today.

RACHEL: What you mean, they want his resignation?

DEACON LORDE: The board is having a meeting at the church as we speak. Deaconess Jones already has a new pastor in mind.

RACHEL: Well, you get down there Deacon Lorde. See if you can stop it?

DEACON LORDE: Don't you understand? There is nothing I can do. They don't need my vote to do it. It doesn't have to be unanimous to get rid of Rev, just the majority vote.

RACHEL: Jacob is in his study. I guess you can go on up and tell him what's going on.

DEACON LORDE: I can't. I can't do it. I think he would take it better if it came from you. Yeah, I'm the head Deacon, but I don't want to be the one to tell him that all of his years of hard work have blown up in smoke. He'll think I had something to do with it, and I didn't. I think this news will come better from someone he loves .

(*Deacon Lorde exits. Rachel returns to the study as if she's seen a ghost.*)

REV. JACOB CROSS: Who was that?

RACHEL: Deacon Lorde.

REV. JACOB CROSS: You can tell him, I'm in the study. We can talk about us later.

RACHEL: He already left.

REV. JACOB CROSS: Left? Well, what did he want?

RACHEL: He came to tell you that the church wants your resignation this afternoon. They know you took over $50,000 from the church Sick-and-Shut-in fund. I guess that was the last straw Jacob. (*Pause.*) Now its time for you to come clean and tell me what's going on.

(*There is a long pause. Jacob pushes the books off his desk, pounds his fist on it, and sits in his chair*).

REV. JACOB CROSS: No more lies Rachel. No more lies. I've been hiding long enough. Quite frankly, I'm tired of running. (*Pause.*) About a year into our marriage, I had and affair with Sister Deborah Woods.

RACHEL: Sister Woods, but isn't she married?

REV. JACOB CROSS: Yes, she was.

RACHEL: Oh my Lord.

REV. JACOB CROSS: I was counseling her and somehow I got caught up. You had just had Solomon. Things were different between us. I mean when I looked at you, I didn't see a wife. I saw a mother. With the late night feedings and all the exhaustion of parenting, we just weren't having any fun anymore and of course our sex life, it became no existent. The next thing I knew Deborah, I mean Sister Woods and I were having lunch together, going to movies, and soon we were sleeping together. It was one of the biggest mistakes of my life.

RACHEL: Oh Jacob. I trusted you. All these years I walked around feeling safe, feeling like you weren't the kind of man who would do such a thing. You were always so noble acting. Yeah, I thought you were the exception. Mama always told me not to trust a man as far as I could throw him. Boy, I was bent on proving to her there were a few good men out there. When I walked down the aisle on the arms of a minister, I thought I was safe. I was the Mrs. to Reverend Jacob Cross an ordained good man. And now I see you ain't no different then the rest of the dogs out here. I guess all men are weak, ministers or not.

REV. JACOB CROSS: That was the only affair that I have ever had, Rachel. Please believe me. I've never been with any other woman. It was hard to live with myself knowing that I was an adulterer, the very sin I spent so many Sunday's warning the congregation against.

RACHEL: You're not only an adulterer, but you're a liar Jacob. (*Long pause.*)

REV. JACOB CROSS: Look, I know that you're mad.

RACHEL: No I'm not mad. I'm furious Why couldn't you tell me, tell me that we were disconnecting back then? You're always harping about communication. Why couldn't you just communicate?

REV. JACOB CROSS: You were always so busy.

RACHEL: Oh, you're not going to turn this thing around on me. You're the one who was out here unzipping your pants for women in the congregation. This whole time, I've been living under the illusion that we were a good family. You've lied to me. What else don't I know about you?

REV. JACOB CROSS: There is more.

RACHEL: More?

REV. JACOB CROSS: Deborah is black mailing me. I had to pay her $50,000 to keep quiet.

RACHEL: Is that why you took the money? So you go and drag the church even further into this mess? $50,000 for an affair that you had twenty some years ago?

REV. JACOB CROSS: No, I fathered a child with her, a girl.

RACHEL: A child? Jacob how could you?

REV. JACOB CROSS: I've never paid one dime of child support or even acknowledged the child. That's why I didn't come to you sooner. I felt obligated to pay her the money.

RACHEL: Jesus keep me near the cross. Grandma always told me that what was done in the dark would soon come to light and lord was she right. *(Slight laugh.)* I can't say I haven't been warned. It all makes sense that dream I had a couple of months ago. Solomon being in the accident and breaking his legs. Goodman the keyboardist walking out without a scratch, and you losing the church. I saw that when the girl stepped on your minister's collar. It was your daughter who was holding your hand in that dream.
(Pause.) I don't see how I could go and ever forgive you for this.

REV. JACOB CROSS: Well, God said we're supposed to forgive.

RACHEL: Look don't you go throwing what God said up in my face. You ain't got no room to be preaching to nobody with the way you been carrying on. I've always tried to be a good wife to you. I've washed your dirty draws, ironed your clothes, drawn you bathwater, cooked you favorite meals. And never once was I unfaithful to you. I was never even tempted. And for all this, what did I get out of it? Nothing but embarrassment. You think it's easy to be your wife, with your pride, your arrogance; giving up my dream of owning a catering business, so I could be a good first lady at the church. Do you even know where that child is now Jacob?

REV. JACOB CROSS: You're not going to believe this, but it's Destiny?

RACHEL: Don't go trying to pretend that God had anything to do with planning this jumbled mess.

REV. JACOB CROSS: No, it's Destiny, Solomon's physical therapist. I didn't even know who she was or what she looked like 'til Deborah gave me a picture. She doesn't even know I'm her father.

RACHEL: Oh my God, Solomon. That explains why the little girl was wearing the nurse's uniform. He's fallen for that girl Jacob. You better hope to heaven that haven't been intimate. You should have told me sooner. I wouldn't have encouraged them. You've got to tell them before it gets to be too late.

REV. JACOB CROSS: We can tell them tomorrow.

RACHEL: I ain't going to tell them nothing. This is your mess. I'm not going to help you get out of this one. Do you think we're just going to go on with our lives like nothing ever happened? We're just supposed to eat dinner, go to bed, and wake up tomorrow and then do it all again. I don't think so Jacob. I don't think so. I don't think I can go on being the sweet dependable Rachel this time. I aught to leave your ... (*She stops herself*)! I just, I just, I just can't look at you anymore.

(*Rachel runs out of the room. Solomon has been listening for most of the conversation. He busts in the study to confront his father.*)

SOLOMON: Do you see how much pain you've caused dad? Deacon Lorde had to come by here to tell you that you lost the church 'cause you stole money? Deuteronomy 5:19: Though Shall not steal. Do you remember that commandment dad? And Destiny, your illegitimate love child who I was getting into, and I don't mean as a brother. Incest would have looked real good on the family tree.

Deuteronomy 5:18 though shall not commit adultery. Do you remember that commandment dad? And then there is your wife, who's been there for you all these years. She's cooked and cleaned and been the perfect wife and mother, who you've lied to for all of your entire marriage. Deuteronomy 5: 20: Though shall not lie. Do you remember that commandment Dad? And then there's me, your son who's looked up to you, who you always made feel unworthy, like I could never measure up to a fine upright Christian man like you. And you, you, you're just a big disappointment.

REV. JACOB CROSS: I may have been all those things, Solomon. I may have been a liar; I may have been an adulterer, I may have been a thief, but no matter what, I am still your father. And you will respect me and honor me.

SOLOMON: Yeah, that's right. Deuteronomy 5:16: Honor your mother and father and your days will be longer. You think God had a man like you in mind when he wrote that commandment? (*Jacob backslaps him and Solomon grabs his coat and exits.*)

Intermission

Act II

Scene 1: How Long?

Rachel shares her feelings with her husband.

Two weeks later, Jacob is at home alone. His house is a wreck, and he is still trying to call Rachel at her sister's house. Jacob looks unkempt.

(The doorbell rings. It's Deacon Lorde)

REV. JACOB CROSS: Come on in Deacon Lorde.

DEACON LORDE: Rev.? *(He looks around the room, steps over the junk and is shocked.)* I guess Rachel still ain't home yet is she?

REV. JACOB CROSS: I told you. You don't have to call me Rev . I'm not your pastor anymore.

DEACON LORDE: You'll always be my pastor, Rev. I ain't been back at the church since you left. What you did was wrong Rev., but, what the church did was worse. They didn't even give you the opportunity to plead your case. You were the founding pastor. Many of the members on the board weren't even around when you struggled to get the church going. Did you know Deaconess Jones, got her nephew as the acting pastor? He ain't but 28-years old. They should have made some exceptions for you. (*Pause.*) Hey, why don't you start another church? We can start back all over again at the Chicken Shack. It'll be like old times. Now that was excitement, watching the church grow.

REV. JACOB CROSS: Deac. that was over 30 years ago. I'm not a young man anymore. We're not young men. I don't have the energy or the stamina to withstand all the aggravation or as you call it, excitement. Besides, I have different priorities now. I got to get my family back. Rachel, she been at her sisters for over two weeks now, and God knows where Solomon is. I really messed up this time.

DEACON LORDE: Yeah you did. But it'll work out.

REV. JACOB CROSS: I've got to make it work out. I can't go on living without them.

DEACON LORDE: (*Looking around.*) I see that. Man you want me to call a maid service for you?

REV. JACOB CROSS: I'll get to it. Cleaning this place was on the top of my to-do list today?

DEACON LORDE: What else is on that list?

REV. JACOB CROSS: Finding a job.

DEACON LORDE: A job?

REV. JACOB CROSS: Yeah, I don't have a salary anymore. I've got just enough money saved to last me another month. Then my pot is empty. I don't know what I'm a do.

DEACON LORDE: Well how did you support yourself before you were a pastor?

REV. JACOB CROSS You know I was a brick mason, but these 55-year-old bones can't stand the heat or cold like I could when I was in my twenty's.

DEACON LORDE: Well then, there you go. That means you should go ahead and start another church.

REV. JACOB CROSS: I can't do that. I don't even have the same passion I had before. I have to face it. The anointing has been off me for a while now. He got me, the devil has got me exactly where he wants me.

DEACON LORDE: You shouldn't say that. It ain't over Rev. It ain't over. You still got today. I shouldn't have to ask you this, but I will. Have you prayed about it?

REV. JACOB CROSS: No, I haven't. God don't bless mess. I got myself into this; now I got to get myself out.

DEACON LORDE: No Rev. Naw. Where is your faith?

REV. JACOB CROSS: My faith doesn't have anything to do with it. You think God is going to forgive what I've done? I mean, I was the leader, the Shepard. I've done some bad things, probably even worse than the folks in the congregation. I guess you could call me the Lost Shepard now.

DEACON LORDE: Remember that sermon you preached about Satan's tricks? You talked about how he wants us to stay focused on the past so we can't see our future. Do you remember that Rev? You had the church shouting that Sunday. Sister Jackson got so happy she twisted her ankle (*chuckling*). That Sunday, I was set free of some things, a lot of people in the church were. You still got a future Rev.

REV. JACOB CROSS: Yeah, I remember that (*Smile*). That was when I was still anointed.

DEACON LORDE: Whether you are anointed now or not, the Word is still the same. Jesus will forgive you of your mistakes if you ask him. You got to be willing to forgive yourself. Then you can move forward.

REV. JACOB CROSS: You think Destiny will ever forgive me?

DEACON LORDE: Have you asked her?

REV. JACOB CROSS: Asked her, I haven't even told her? How do I tell that grown woman that her father, a married man, a pastor at that was the one who forsook her and her mother all those years ago?

DEACON LORDE: Seems like it's the perfect time to make that move. Way I see it, you really ain't got nothing to lose. How far can you fall from the bottom?

REV. JACOB CROSS: Not far at all.

DEACON LORDE: I suggest you get on that phone and call her. Tell her you need to talk to her.

REV. JACOB CROSS: You know, I think I'll do that. (*He goes to an end table and pulls out an address book.*) I think Rachel keeps all the important numbers in here. Here it is Destiny Woods. (*He gets on the phone, dials, then speaks.*) Yes, may I speak to Destiny? Destiny, this is Reverend, I mean, Mr. Cross. Do you think you would be able to come by later, say 6:00? After you finish your rounds is fine. Yeah I need to discuss some things with you. I'd rather talk to you in person. Alright, I'll see you then.

DEACON LORDE: I'll help you get this place cleaned up.

REV. JACOB CROSS: Deacon Lorde, (*Pause.*) thank you. You're a friend that's closer than a brother.

(*The place is cleaned by Deacon Lorde and Jacob. Deacon Lorde exits, Jacob has cleaned himself up, as Deacon Lorde leaves, Destiny arrives*)

DESTINY: Rev. Cross, I was surprised to get a call from you. Have you heard from Solomon?

REV. JACOB CROSS: No, not yet. Look, I didn't call you to discuss Solomon exactly. I asked you to come here so I could talk about you.

DESTINY: About me?

REV. JACOB CROSS: Yes, can I get you something to drink, a snack? I think I have some chips and soda.

DESTINY: No thank you. (*Destiny feels awkward.*) This isn't about billing is it? You have to talk to the hospital billing department about that. I had to go ahead and bill Solomon for the missed sessions. That's hospital policy.

REV. JACOB CROSS: No, I didn't want to discuss Solomon's therapy bills.

DESTINY: Well this isn't about me not wanting to date Solomon anymore, is it?

REV. JACOB CROSS: You told Solomon you weren't interested in him romantically?

DESTINY: Yeah.

REV. JACOB CROSS: Good.

DESTINY: You don't approve of me with your son?

REV. JACOB CROSS: Destiny, I could beat around the bush, but I guess it is best for me to come right out and say it. Look, I'm your father.

DESTINY: My father? (*Pause.*) My Father?

REV. JACOB CROSS: Yes, I am your father.

(*Pause.*)

DESTINY: I guess that explains it.

REV. JACOB CROSS: Explains what?

DESTINY: Why it didn't feel right with Solomon. (*Destiny goes weak, she readjusts herself in her seat.*)

REV. JACOB CROSS: Destiny are you o.k.?

DESTINY: This isn't the way I imagined I'd find out who my father was.

REV. JACOB CROSS: No this ain't what I imagined either.

DESTINY: I have so many questions. I just don't know where to start.

REV. JACOB CROSS: Look I …

DESTINY: How did y'all meet, y'all both being married and you a pastor?

REV. JACOB CROSS: I was counseling your mother weekly and one thing led to another. Didn't your mother tell you?

DESTINY: She wouldn't tell me one thing except that after you found out she was pregnant, you didn't want to see her ever again. She never told me who you were, only that you were an important man. She knew if the news became public, she would catch all the blame from the community. Women are always held more accountable then men in these situations. She wasn't ready for that in her condition. She did not want to risk a miscarriage. She said you rejected us so badly, I was better off not even knowing you. Why? Why didn't you come and find me when I was younger?

REV. JACOB CROSS: I was so busy trying to cover my own butt, protect my position as a pastor and my marriage that I failed to do the right thing by you. It didn't help any that we were both married. I, at least, didn't want to further interfere with your mother's marriage.

DESTINY: But you did. Soon after dad found out I wasn't his, he split. Those were some rough times. Mama was always crying around the house. When she wasn't working, she'd lock herself up in her room. I always felt responsible for her unhappiness. I wasn't worthy enough for my biological father to want me, and I wasn't good enough for the man who I thought was my father to stick around.

REV. JACOB CROSS: I was wrong. Things would have been a lot different if I would have been honest from the get go. I'm sorry that I've never been the father that you wanted me to be, but I see, I see your mother did a fine job with you. You're smart and a very attractive young woman. You were brought up better than if I would have raised you. I was always so busy with the church that I neglected my family.

DESTINY: It was so hard on her. She had to work two jobs just to make ends meet. Oh Uncle Billy and Aunt Tangy tried their best to fill in the gaps, be a father to me; but it just wasn't the same. I spent so many nights dreaming about what my father would look like. Would he be tall and thin, short and fat? Would he have a head full of hair, would he be bald? I used to dream about being in a gorgeous overflowing gown like Cinderella, coming down a set of spiraling stairs; and there would be my father standing, looking, and admiring me, telling me I was beautiful, telling me I was somebody.(*Pause.)*

REV. JACOB CROSS: Look I know I've missed out on a lot, and I would like to be that father to you now, if you'd have me. Do you think you could ever forgive me?

DESTINY: Did you even love mama?

REV. JACOB CROSS: I cared about her very much.

DESTINY: You cared so much you let her go to Chicago and never contacted us again?

REV. JACOB CROSS: I didn't know where she had gone. When she left, I never heard from her again 'til recently. I never even knew what you looked like 'til I got a picture of you a few weeks ago. Boy was I shocked to find out you were right up under my nose the whole time, right under my roof, helping my son.

DESTINY: So mama contacted you?

REV. JACOB CROSS: Just recently, that's when she gave me your picture.

DESTINY: She must've finally gotten the nerve to tell your wife.

REV. JACOB CROS: She didn't tell Rachel, I did?

DESTINY: Why, why would you want to come clean now?

REV. JACOB CROSS: Your mother was blackmailing me. I paid her $50,000 to keep quiet. I got desperate and made the mistake of taking the money from the church and ended up losing my position anyway. Once the church found out what I'd done, I had to tell Rachel.

DESTINY: I'm not going to sit here and let you lie on my mother like this.

REV. JACOB CROSS: Look, I'm not trying to cause a rift between you and your mother. I'll let you talk to your mother about all this.

DESTINY: And Solomon and Mrs. Cross, how do they feel about all this? (*Pause.*)

REV. JACOB CROSS: They left, but it wasn't about you Destiny. They're mad at me for lying to them.

DESTINY: Look, I got to go. I got a lot to think about all this.

REV. JACOB CROSS: Look Destiny I really would like to see you again.

DESTINY: You know, when I was younger, I would have been thrilled to have you in my life, but now that I'm older, I just don't see where you'd fit in.

(*Destiny looks at him and exits the door. Jacob goes to the sofa and starts reading the classified ads, he is circling jobs of interest.*)

Scene 2: The War

Deacon Lorde gets new information about current circumstances.

(*Jacob exits to the kitchen. Rachel enters once Jacob is in the kitchen. Rachel sets down her luggage. Jacob re-enters carrying a snack. He sets it down quickly when he sees her.*)

REV. JACOB CROSS: Rachel, you're back?

RACHEL: I think you knew deep down I wasn't going to be gone forever.

REV. JACOB CROSS: Does this mean that you forgive me?

RACHEL: I wouldn't say I'm there. It was time for me to come back home. Jackie got to acting more like my mama than my sister. You're not off the hook yet Jacob Cross.

REV. JACOB CROSS: Well, are you hungry? Can I get you something?

RACHEL: I could use a hot bath and something to eat.

REV. JACOB CROSS: I just fixed myself a sandwich, but you can eat it.

RACHEL: I had something in mind a lot hotter than that.

REV. JACOB CROSS: Now we talkin'.

RACHEL: Oh, you can just forget about that. Forget about that for a long while.

REV. JACOB CROSS: How long you go'n be mad at me, one more week, another month, a year, two years?

RACHEL: Look, you think I want to feel the way that I do? I don't even have the energy for this right now. I'm going to get in the tub.

REV. JACOB CROSS: I was wrong Rachel. I admit that. It was 23 years ago. It's done. Destiny's here, and there is nothing we can do about that now. We can't turn back time.

RACHEL: This is the only time in the history of our marriage that I wish; I just wish I had never married you.

REV. JACOB CROSS: But you did marry me. We are married. We gone keep on being married unless you thinking about getting a divorce.

RACHEL: Don't think it hasn't crossed my mind these past few weeks. I've thought about it. I've thought about it a lot. But even still, I don't think I'm ready to throw it all away. I've put a lot of work into helping us get what we have. It's going to take time. All the trust that I had has vanished. We've got to start all over again.

REV. JACOB CROSS: I'm willing to do that. Especially if it means being with you.

RACHEL: You just get me something to eat.

REV. JACOB CROSS: I'll have it ready for you by the time you get out the tub.

(*Rachel exits to her room. Jacob cuts on the tv and hangs out a little while on the couch. Goodman comes to the door.*)

REV. JACOB CROSS: Goodman, I'm sorry Solomon isn't here. He hasn't been home for a couple of weeks now.

GOODMAN: I know. That's why I'm here. Solomon has been staying with me.

REV. JACOB CROSS: He has?

GOODMAN: Yes sir. Reverend Cross I came to give you some news.

REV. JACOB CROSS: What, has something happened to Solomon?

GOODMAN: He's run off and joined the Army?

REV. JACOB CROSS: The Army?

GOODMAN: Yes, he said he couldn't take staying here any longer. He told me about Destiny. He took the news really badly.

REV. JACOB CROSS: I don't think the Army is going to take him, him having a bad leg and all. I am not going to worry about it too much.

GOODMAN: You don't understand. His leg is completely healed.

REV. JACOB CROSS: What you mean completely healed? When he left out of here a few weeks ago, he was hobbling.

GOODMAN: I know. The day you had the argument, he showed up on my doorstep real upset. He was in such pain; he could barely make it through the door.

REV. JACOB CROSS: Did Destiny finish her sessions with him?

GOODMAN: As far as I know, he hasn't seen Destiny since he's been at my house. He came to my church the following Sunday. Sir, does your church lay hands?

REV. JACOB CROSS: No.

GOODMAN: Well my pastor is anointed. Several have come to him sick and left well.

REV. JACOB CROSS: You mean Solomon went to church with you? He hasn't been to church since he was 13.

GOODMAN: He went gladly. He was a desperate looking for answers. Pastor Hilman had an alter call at the end of the sermon. He placed his hands on Solomon's bad leg. Solomon walked out of that church healed in the name of Jesus. He said he was walking better than before his leg was injured. His leg was good enough for him to pass the physical for the Army, Reverend Cross.

REV. JACOB CROSS: Really?

GOODMAN: I tried to talk him out of it. In light of everything that is going on in the country. I have a feeling we're about to go to war.

REV. JACOB CROSS: War?

GOODMAN: Yes war.

REV. JACOB CROSS: I guess I've been so engrossed with what was going on in my own life that I haven't been paying much attention to what's going on in the world.

GOODMAN: Well, President Bush is about to declare war on Iraq. He's making a speech tonight. Many already think it's a done deal. The good news is many think it will be a two-month operation at most. Our military capabilities and armed forces greatly out power theirs.

REV. JACOB CROSS: A two-month operation? Solomon may not get through basic training before it's over.

GOODMAN: Let's pray so.

REV. JACOB CROSS: How am I going to tell his mother?

GOODMAN: Reverend Cross, I'm sorry to hear about everything that's been going on with your church and your family. I imagine it must be pretty tough. Satan is always busy you know. I guess I don't have to tell you to just put on the armor of God.

REV. JACOB CROSS: Goodman, thank you for taking the time to let me know. You don't happen to know where he will be stationed?

GOODMAN: Fayetteville, Fayetteville North Carolina at Fort Bragg.

REV. JACOB CROSS: At least it's not too far away. Maybe when things cool off a bit, his mother and I can go and visit him. You have a good night. And Solomon, say a prayer for us.

GOODMAN: (*Exiting.*) I'll do that. I'll especially say a prayer for you pastor.

(*Jacob exits to the kitchen. Rachel comes down putting lotion on her hands in her bathrobe.*)

RACHEL: Jacob, I thought I heard somebody at the door. Who was it? Jacob? (*Talking to herself.*) I know he still ain't cookin'. (*She cuts up the volume on the TV. She drifts* *off to sleep. President Bush's address can be heard on the television. He talks about there will be body bags etc… Jacob comes in with a plate and a soda.)*

REV. JACOB CROSS: *(Waking her.)* Rachel, Rachel, I got your food ready. Rachel?

RACHEL: *(She startles.)* Oh, Jacob. I just had a dream. It's the third time this week. I saw Solomon in military fatigues. He was running and then all of a sudden there is this big explosion and everything goes black.

REV. JACOB CROSS: Did you know that Solomon was with Goodman?

RACHEL: I figured he was with Goodman. I sure hope they staying out of trouble.

REV. JACOB CROSS: Rachel, Goodman came by to tell us that Solomon joined the Army. Goodman said his leg was healed. He went to church with him, and Pastor Hilman touched his leg in the name of Jesus. Solomon was healed by the time he left the church.

RACHEL: Ohh my Lord. Oh God Jacob. That explains my dream. What's next?   What do you suppose it meant when everything went black after the explosion I saw ? *(Talking to God.)* What did I do? What did I do to get punished like this?

REV. JACOB CROSS: You ain't done nothing.

RACHEL: *(Rachel faints. Jacob gets her some smelling sauce to bring her to. Whispering out of delusion.)* Solomon.

REV. JACOB CROSS: Rachel you need to get in the bed. It'll help clear your head so you can think straight. (*Rachel begins to exit to her room.*)

RACHEL: You better hope that don't nothing happen to that boy. You just better pray nothing don't happen to Solomon.

(*He escorts Rachel to her room and then re-enters the living room goes out to the mail box and enters again with mail.*)

Scene 3: The Vote

Deacon Lorde, Destiny, Rachel, and Rev. Cross discuss the vote.

REV. JACOB CROSS: (*Shuffling through the mail.*) Rachel's, junk, junk, junk, bills, bills, bills, junk, Rachel's hmmm Bloomberg Bank and Trust. (*He opens it and looks at it.*) Woo. (*He jumps up and down.*) Thank you Jesus. Thank you Jesus. (*Rachel rushes in from the kitchen.*)

RACHEL: What? What is it?

REV. JACOB CROSS: Rachel honey it's a miracle. Can you believe it? Can you believe it? Is it real? I must be dreaming (*Hands it to her.*)

RACHEL: Naw you ain't dreaming Jacob. That's a check for $60,000!

REV. JACOB CROSS: Give me the envelope. Let me read it again "Dear Mr. Cross: Enclosed are the dividends for the B.I.G. MART Stock purchased in 1967…" I had forgotten all about that stock. Lord you may not come when we want you, but you be there right on time.

(The doorbell rings enter Deacon Lorde carrying the church bylaws.)

DEACON LORDE: Rachel glad to see you home. Where Rev?

RACHEL: He's right there on the sofa.

DEACON LORDE: Rev. I got some good news.

REV. JACOB CROSS: Me too.

DEACON LORDE: My news first. I've been studying the church by-laws all week. The board did not have the right to dismiss you like that.

REV. JACOB CROSS: What?

DEACON LORDE: I said the board did not have the right to dismiss you. Listen to this. This is Article VII, Section 3 of the Church By-Laws. (*Reading*) "The pastor shall be chosen and dismissed by vote of the church at any legal meeting, provided that notice of such intended action shall have been inserted in the call of such meeting. A vote of at least three-fourths of the members present shall be required to call or dismiss a pastor." Don't you see? They violated two rules in article VII.

REV. JACOB CROSS: They did?

DEACON LORDE: Yeah you didn't hear which ones?

REV. JACOB CROSS: I'm afraid you're going to have to break it down to me.

DEACON LORDE: First of all, the meeting was not a legal meeting. It was not announced to the church properly via insert into the church program or mailer. Second, what members did come, they went with the majority of the votes. They did not receive three-fourths of the votes of the members present. I think we have reason for a recall. I'm gone get on the phone and call Deaconess Jones this minute.

REV. JACOB CROSSL: Before you do that, I've got some good news.

DEACON LORDE: It can't be any better than what I just told you.

REV. JACOB CROSS: Oh, it's better.

DEACON LORDE: Out with it Rev.

REV. JACOB CROSS: Look what I just received in the mail. (Jacob hands the check to Deacon Lorde.).

DEACON LORDE: This here, this is a check for $60,000. Where in the world did that come from?

REV. JACOB CROSS: Would you believe that? Over thirty years ago, I bought some stock in Big Mart. I had forgotten all about it. Today, I looked in the mailbox, and there set this check for my dividends.

DEACON LORDE: You know what this means don't you?

REV. JACOB CROSS: You bet I do.

DEACON LORDE: You 'bout to put that money back in the Sick-and-Shut-in fund.

REV. JACOB CROSS: Yeah, I sure am.

DEACON LORDE: I got to call Deaconess Jones this minute. I can't wait to hear what she says. Can I use your phone?

REV. JACOB CROSS: You don't even need to ask.

DEACON LORDE: Yes hello, this Deaconess Jones? Deaconess Jones this is Deacon Lorde. Look I been reviewing the church bylaws. And according to it, Rev. Cross was unlawfully dismissed. Yes that's right. It's right there in Article VII, Section3. Yeah, I'll hold while you get your copy. (*Talking to Rev. Cross*). She going to get her copy. This is great. (*Talking to Deaconess Jones.*) A vote of at least three-fourths of the members present shall be required to call or dismiss a pastor. Look we didn't have a legal meeting. We didn't announce the meeting properly; and second of all, we went with the majority vote of the church, not three-fourths which means we got to have a revote. Oh yeah, what are you going to tell the church about the grounds? Oh there is no money missing from the sick and shut-in fund. In fact, there is $10,000 more than what was originally there. I don't care if it was missing at one time, its back in there now, in less than 30 days. Yeah call the board. I will challenge you on it. Oh and you can tell that nephew of yours that he'll

need to find another church to takeover, I mean pastor.
Well, you have a good day too. (*He hangs up the phone.*)
We got 'em Rev. We got'em right where we want them. Get your favorite robe pressed and your sermon ready. I have a feeling this whole thing will be over in less than a week.

REV. JACOB CROSS: Oh this is good news. Thank you Lord.

DEACON LORDE: You're welcome.

REV. JACOB CROSS: I was thanking the savior.

DEACON LORDE: Now Rev. it's all looking better. Now I'm not saying everything is going to be hunky dory. You are going to lose some members behind this. But at least you won't have to start all over again.

RACHEL: If only Solomon were home, then things would be better.
He's joined the Army, you know.

DEACON LORDE: With that bum leg?

REV. JACOB CROSS: He was healed by Pastor Hilman.

DEACON LORDE: (*Catches the Spirit*) That's bittersweet news. On the one hand his leg is healed, but on the other he picked the worst possible time to join the Army --The War on Terrorism.

REV. JACOB CROSS: Good news is they say it'll be a quick operation, two months. Solomon probably wouldn't have finished basic training by then.

DEACON LORDE: You think so? I don't know. The way I see it the Muslims are real upset about the whole world order. Many folks say they are going to make this a holy war, the Muslims versus the Christians.

RACHEL: Y'all are scaring me.

DEACON LORDE: I don't mean to scare you Rachel, but it's true. Anytime you have people willing to blow themselves up for the cause, you got to get scared. Men, women and children, all of 'em strappin' themselves with bombs.

RACHEL: We need to just pray. We need to pray for Solomon. We need to pray for the country.

DEACON LORDE: Oh I will. And I'll say a pray for pastor too. He's got his own war right here at home. Be ready to vote next week Rachel. I'll come and pick you up when it's time.

FADE

Scene 4: The Prodigal Son

Solomon returns home.

DEACON LORDE: Rev, I'm sorry. Things didn't go the way we'd hoped.

REV. JACOB CROSS: They voted me out? (*He goes to the phone.*) Maybe I can try to stop the check.

DEACON LORDE: It's too late to get that money. The check already cleared a few days ago.

RACHEL: Where do we go from here Jacob? (Destiny enter through knock at the door)

REV. JACOB CROSS: I don't know how we gonna make it. (*Pause.*)

The phone rings. Jacob goes to answer it.)

Hello. Yes this is Rev. Jacob Cross. You say your name is Sargeant. Michael Collins from the U.S. Army? Oh my God, is he alright. I see. I see. Well is there any way my wife and I can come out to see him? No? His mother is going to be hysterical if she can't. I see. I see. Well thank you for calling.

Rachel, Sergeant Collins called from the Army. Solomon's been in an explosion.

RACHEL: Lord, help!

REV. JACOB CROSS: Look, he is in stable condition, but he has lost his sight. The doctors said that he may not see again.

RACHEL: Well let's get packed. Let's go see him.

REV. JACOB CROSS: We can't.

RACHEL: Why, he oversees?

REV. JACOB CROSS: No, at Fort Bragg.

RACHEL: Jacob, that's just one state down in North Carolina. If we leave now, we can be there before nighttime.

REV. JACOB CROSS: Rachel, he is not accepting any visitors.

RACHEL: What is that military policy?

REV. JACOB CROSS: No, he specifically asked that we not see him.

RACHEL: What?

(*Destiny gathers her things as she is about to dash*).

REV. JACOB CROSS: Destiny where you going?

DESTINY: I'm on my way to get Goodman. He didn't say anything about us not seeing him.

RACHEL: You're wasting your time, they probably will only let family in.

DESTINY: Well I am his sister.

(*She exits.*)

RACHEL: Jacob Antonio Cross, see what you've done to my baby?

(*She exits to the bedroom. The audience hears a door slam.*).

DEACON LORDE: Well Rev.

REV. JACOB CROSS: Deacon Lorde please. I can't stand to beat myself up about this. Nobody told that boy to run off to the military. He's always trying to run from his problems
When do they want my resignation?

DEACON LORDE: As far as they're concerned, they'll accept the resignation from the first vote.

DEACON LORDE: They would like the robes and minister collars. They do belong to the church.

REV. JACOB CROSS: They're not trying to leave me with one crumb are they?

DEACON LORDE: I guess not. Look, you want me to take them? That way you don't even have to go down there and look at nobody

REV. JACOB CROSS: No, I'm not going to duck and hide. I'll take it down there myself.

DEACON LORDE: Look Rev., you call me if you need me, and I do mean for anything? (*Deacon Lorde exits*.).

(*Rev. Cross sits on the couch and looks around bewildered and sad. Then he gets up and exits to his study and looks at his ministers robes and collars. He takes one and puts it on.*)

Fade

Scene 5: In My Father's House

Rev. Cross returns to his church.

Jacob is at his former church and is returning his things while confessing to God in front of a huge cross.

REV. JACOB CROSS *(Before the Cross)*: Well lord, this is it, the point of no return. I had a test, and I failed it. I failed my wife, I failed my son, I failed my daughter, and I failed the church. I failed you God. I'd like to think when it's my time, I would have learned my lessons and lived right, made you proud. I guess you're pretty disappointed now. (*He goes up to the pulpit chair and places his robes and collar on the pastor's chair.*) I guess, I'm wondering what now. Where do I go from here? Have I done so much wrong that I can't be used? (*Pause, hearing a sound*) Who's there? Deacon Lorde, that you? (*Pause *addressing God again.*) The weird thing is I thought I was smart, thought I had the power to cover it all up, you know erase it? But I see I just made one big mess, a mess that I can't clean up. I guess I've learned that when I have a problem to come to you and let you handle it, not pray and then take the wheel. (*There is a stumble sound again.*) Deacon Lorde? (*Appearing from the corner comes Solomon staggering in the darkness with his cane.*) Solomon? (*Surprised*) Let me help you son.

SOLOMON: No, I've got it.

REV. JACOB CROSS: What you doing down here at the church? It's after midnight?

SOLOMON: I was going to ask you the same thing. Pastor Hilman had a revival. I thought I could go down there, he'd lay hands on me and I'd have my sight back. But it didn't work out that way. Guess I'm stuck like this forever. (*Pause*) So, I guess I'm up here doing the same as you, looking for answers.

REV. JACOB CROSS: Son, don't give up. Pastor Hilman don't have no power to heal, only Jesus does. (*Pause.*) You think you gone find it here, the answers you looking for?

SOLOMON: Don't know.

REV. JACOB CROSS: Solomon, I was real sorry to hear about what happened to your sight. Well, I mean, the only thing I can say to you is that I'm sorry. I'm sorry for the lies and the deceit. Real men don't lie to the people that they love. I really let you and your mother down. I know that there is nothing I can do to make it up to you. But no mater what you think, I was doing what I thought was right. I wanted to be a good example to you. I wanted you to be the man that I always wanted to be.

(*Solomon chuckles*)

REV. JACOB CROSS: What's funny?

SOLOMON: That was the topic of Pastor Hilman's sermon.

REV. JACOB CROSS: What?

SOLOMON: Perfection. He said the only perfect man is Christ. He's the only man who has managed to walk the Earth without making mistakes. If we live, keep on living, we will make mistakes. But through Jesus, we can be forgiven and be set free. If we want Jesus to forgive us though, we got to forgive others. It's the only way God will listen to our prayers, and we will get blessed.

REV. JACOB CROSS: Sounds like that Hilman is a pretty good teacher. I could have used that sermon myself tonight.

SOLOMON: Goodman asked me if I would be the drummer in his Gospel band. Think there is room for someone like me?

REV. JACOB CROSS: What you mean someone like you? You been playing drums since you was six-years old. Bet you can play them in your sleep.

(*Long pause*)

SOLOMON: Daddy, I forgive you.

REV. JACOB CROSS: You forgive me? Oh thank you son. You don't know what that does for my soul. (*They hug and embrace. He falls down on his knees, pulling Solomon with him as he thanks Jesus and weeps.*) Oh thank you Jesus. God you're so good. You're so mighty. You're so steadfast. I praise and bless your name Jesus. Only at the cross. Only at the cross.

Curtain

Psalm 103
Of David.
[1]Praise the Lord, O my soul;
all my inmost being, praise his holy name.
[2]Praise the Lord, O my soul,
and forget not all his benefits-
[3]who forgives all your sins
and heals all your diseases,
[4]who redeems your life from the pit,
and crowns you with love and
compassion,
[5]who satisfies your desires with good things
so that your youth is renewed like the
eagle's.
              --Bible (NIV)

Live!

Watch *A Date with Destiny: It's Hot 'N Heavy* in front of a live studio audience on Amazon Instant Video or order a DVD.

Listen to a dramatic reading on Audible.

Both Coming May 2016

Other Read it, Watch it Books by 2M Entertainments, LLC

Seeing Faith: When Life Throws You Curves

http://amzn.com/B01BMYMR3K

Seeing Faith Summary

Since she can remember, Faith has been bullied about her weight. If it wasn't her school friends, it was her mother. Now the teasing has even leaked into her relationship by a man who is supposed to love her, her fiancé, Esau. She has tried everything to lose the weight including skipping meals altogether, but nothing seems to work. In fact, her wedding dress has been let out so many times, she might to have buy a whole new one. Her inability to lose weight and her frequent binges could be due to the fact that she suspects her fiancé is using her. Though he constantly makes negative comments about her weight, he loves all of the perks that come along with dating the boss' daughter. While traveling with him on a business trip to Jamaica, she realizes that the slender ideal she was taught in America does not exist everywhere. In fact, her curves are a benefit instead of a disadvantage. While Esau works, Faith spends most of her free time with Hosea, a Jamaican architect who likes a woman with meat on her bones. Will Esau win Faith's affections again or will he lose to Hosea? What happens when a plus-size woman starts to value her curves? Find out in Seeing Faith: When Life Throws You Curves

Watch the *Seeing Faith* on Amazon Instant Video or order a DVD.

Listen to a dramatic reading on Audible.com. Coming May 2016.

Watch Seeing Faith Trailer:
https://www.youtube.com/watch?v=saxgOkIURRw

www.ingramcontent.com/pod-product-compliance
Lightning Source LLC
LaVergne TN
LVHW051509070426
835507LV00022B/3005